# The Silent Architect: A Biography of Susie Wiles

*Unveiling the Power Moves Behind America's Political Landscape*

Ethan Reynolds

© 2024 by [Ethan Reynolds]

All rights reserved. No part of this publication may be reproduced, distributed, or transmitted in any form or by any means, including photocopying, recording, or other electronic or mechanical methods, without the prior written permission of the publisher, except in the case of brief quotations embodied in critical reviews and certain other noncommercial uses permitted by copyright law.

# Table of Contents

Prologue: A Legacy in the Shadows ............................................... 4

Chapter 1: Early Influences and Formative Years .................... 10

Chapter 2: Breaking into Politics ................................................ 15

Chapter 3: Navigating the Local Arena ..................................... 21

Chapter 4: The 2010 Florida Gubernatorial Campaign ............ 28

Chapter 5: Joining Trump's 2016 Campaign ............................ 34

Chapter 6: The 2020 Re-Election Battle .................................... 41

Chapter 7: Power and Controversy ........................................... 47

Chapter 8: The Split with DeSantis ............................................ 54

Chapter 9: The Return to Trump and 2024 ............................... 61

Chapter 10: First Woman Chief of Staff .................................... 68

Chapter 11: Personal Life and Legacy ....................................... 75

Chapter 12: Reflections and Lessons ......................................... 81

Epilogue: The Lasting Impact of a Power Broker ..................... 88

# Prologue: A Legacy in the Shadows

In American politics, where public recognition often signals power, Susie Wiles stands as an enigmatic force whose influence has rarely taken center stage. Her career, spanning several decades, has been built not on the blinding lights of fame but on the quiet, calculated moves that shape the nation's most crucial decisions. From her early days in local government to her high-profile roles in national campaigns, Susie has made a name for herself among insiders as a woman who can turn the tide in favor of her candidate without a trace. Many may not know her by name, but her impact reverberates through some of the most pivotal events in recent American history.

Susie's journey into politics wasn't a straightforward ambition. Born in 1957 to Pat Summerall, a beloved NFL player and broadcaster, she was raised in a family familiar with the spotlight but grounded in values of discretion and resilience. Growing up with a father who was both a public figure and a war veteran, Susie learned early on about the balance between maintaining a strong public image and keeping one's private affairs out of view. This upbringing taught her the essential skill of reading people — a talent that would serve her well in the politically charged environments she would later navigate.

Her early years were marked by a keen interest in understanding what drives people. After completing her Bachelor of Arts in English, she found herself drawn to the world of public service. However, unlike many of her contemporaries, Susie didn't enter politics to make her views known or to be in the spotlight. Instead, she was fascinated by the behind-the-scenes mechanisms — the strategies, relationships, and decisions that quietly shaped public opinion. When she began her career as a staff assistant to Representative Jack Kemp, it wasn't long before her talent for strategy and her unique approach to problem-solving caught the attention of key players.

"Susie was one of those rare people you meet who could see five moves ahead in any situation," recalls a former colleague from Kemp's office. "While most of us were busy handling the day-to-day grind, she was already considering what would happen three weeks down the line. That instinct made her an asset — not just to our team but to anyone who understood the value of foresight in politics."

Her aptitude for strategy quickly landed her a spot on Ronald Reagan's 1980 campaign, a groundbreaking opportunity that set the tone for her future in the world of high-stakes political maneuvering. Even in those early years, Susie exhibited a knack for pulling the strings behind the scenes without ever becoming the story herself. This discretion, combined with her analytical mind, led her to positions that allowed her to work directly with top advisors and influencers, reinforcing her reputation as a powerful strategist whose loyalty and skills were as vital as they were understated.

Susie's career took on a new dimension when she moved to Florida in the 1990s. There, she navigated local and state politics with the same quiet determination that had defined her early years. Serving as Chief of Staff to Jacksonville's Mayor John Delaney, she was thrust into the center of policy decisions, budget battles, and media scrutiny — experiences that would prepare her for the heightened pressures of national campaigns. During her time in Florida's political arena, Susie cultivated an approach to politics that was part tactician, part confidante. Her colleagues came to rely on her as a stabilizing force, someone who could navigate even the most polarized situations with calm and foresight.

However, it wasn't until 2010 that Susie's career reached a turning point. That year, she managed Rick Scott's successful gubernatorial campaign in Florida, a feat that caught the attention of strategists and politicians across the country. While Scott's campaign faced numerous obstacles, Susie's strategy was unwavering. She understood that winning in Florida, a politically diverse and critical swing state required not just a sound campaign message but an intricate understanding of the state's unique political landscape. Her work on Scott's campaign solidified her status as one of the most effective operatives in the business, particularly in Florida, where her influence became almost legendary.

"Winning Florida is no small task," says a political analyst familiar with her work. "It's a state that demands precision, and Susie mastered it. She understood the people, the demographics, and the issues that mattered to voters. She took Rick Scott from being an outsider to the Governor of Florida, and that's no easy task, especially in a state as complex as Florida."

But it was her association with Donald Trump's campaigns that would bring her the most recognition — and the most controversy. When she joined Trump's team in 2016, Susie entered a political climate more divisive than any she had previously encountered. Her role was pivotal, yet, true to her nature, she remained largely out of the public eye, crafting strategies that resonated with Florida voters and ultimately contributed to Trump's victory in the state. Despite the charged atmosphere and intense scrutiny, Susie's quiet resilience and focus on the goal at hand became invaluable assets to the campaign. For her, the work was never about personal ideology but about executing a winning strategy.

In many ways, her partnership with Trump was both a culmination of her career and a testament to her adaptability. Working for a candidate as unconventional as Trump required a blend of traditional political wisdom and a willingness to think outside the box. For Susie, it was an opportunity to deploy every skill she had honed over the years, from local governance to national strategy, from quiet diplomacy to handling the intensity of the media. While many of her colleagues found themselves ensnared in controversy or public scandal, Susie's ability to remain effective without courting the limelight allowed her to navigate this period with remarkable composure.

Though her career has been punctuated by achievements that could easily place her among the most famous figures in American politics, Susie Wiles has maintained a life of intentional anonymity. Her influence on some of the nation's most critical elections and her ability to remain under the radar has only added to her mystique. To the few who know her well, Susie's legacy is that of a woman who has mastered the art of subtlety in a world that often rewards boldness. Her career is a testament to the power of quiet authority — the idea that true influence doesn't need to shout.

As the political landscape continues to evolve, so too does Susie's role. In 2024, she stepped into one of her most visible positions yet, co-chairing Trump's campaign and eventually becoming the White House Chief of Staff. For a woman who has built her legacy on remaining out of the spotlight, this role marks a new chapter. Will her influence continue to thrive in an environment where her every move is observed, or will this shift lead to a new understanding of her methods and motivations?

The story of Susie Wiles is one of contrasts — a strategist who thrives in the shadows, a figure with immense influence but little public profile. As her career unfolds, it becomes increasingly clear that her legacy, while often unseen, will leave an indelible mark on American politics. This biography seeks to uncover the layers of her journey, the triumphs, the challenges, and the decisions that have shaped her path and, in many ways, the political path of a nation.

# Chapter 1: Early Influences and Formative Years

For anyone who has ever tried to understand Susie Wiles, it's impossible to ignore the influences of her childhood. Born into a household that balanced public life with a quiet resilience, Susie's earliest years were shaped by her father, Pat Summerall—a man revered as much for his presence in sports broadcasting as for the personal values he instilled in his family. Pat, a former NFL player turned sportscaster, was known across America for his calm and measured voice, which provided the soundtrack to countless football games. But to Susie, he was simply "Dad"—a figure of steadfastness and discipline, who taught her more by action than by words.

Growing up, Susie absorbed the subtle but powerful lessons that came from being the daughter of a public figure. Pat wasn't just a man in the limelight; he was also a World War II veteran and a man deeply committed to his principles. Though he moved comfortably in the public eye, he always carried a sense of duty and humility. Susie watched as her father managed to stay grounded in a world that constantly beckoned him to indulge in the perks of fame. Pat's values—self-control, loyalty, and a focus on the bigger picture—became bedrock principles for Susie. She learned that strength didn't always mean standing in the spotlight; often, it meant making decisions that few would see or understand.

"Dad had this way of teaching us things without really saying them outright," Susie once recalled to a close friend. "He wasn't preachy. He just lived his life a certain way, and we followed."

The Summerall household was unique in that it brought together the excitement of the sports world and the quieter, sometimes intense, discipline Pat expected. Growing up, Susie and her siblings were expected to carry themselves with a sense of responsibility that went beyond their years. Fame and attention, they were reminded, were fleeting, but a reputation for integrity would endure. It was a principle her father held close, one that he demonstrated every time he stepped in front of a microphone or spoke to fans.

In school, Susie was known as a thoughtful, observant child—perhaps even a little reserved. She had an instinct for listening and absorbing the world around her, a skill that would later serve her well in her career. But back then, it simply made her a quiet, inquisitive student. Her teachers often remarked on her ability to see situations from multiple perspectives, a rare quality for someone so young. This early tendency toward empathy, combined with her sense of responsibility, set her apart from her peers.

When it came to her studies, Susie gravitated naturally toward subjects that allowed her to explore the human mind and society. She had a particular affinity for literature and history, which provided her a window into different worlds and experiences. Through books, she discovered how characters navigated complexities and challenges, learning lessons that she would later translate into her own life and career. It was in these pages that she first encountered the idea of subtlety as a form of strength—a theme that would become a hallmark of her professional persona.

During these formative years, her family moved frequently due to her father's broadcasting career, a lifestyle that required adaptability. For Susie, each new environment meant starting fresh, observing, and quickly understanding the unspoken rules of each new school and community. By the time she reached high school, she had developed a keen intuition for reading people—a skill she would one day leverage in the high-stakes world of politics.

But Susie's teenage years were not without their struggles. Watching her father balance his high-profile career with personal challenges—particularly his battle with alcoholism—was a sobering experience. While Pat ultimately overcame his addiction, the impact of those years left a lasting mark on Susie. She saw firsthand the toll that public life could take on an individual and their family. The experience taught her both the value of resilience and the importance of maintaining personal boundaries, lessons that would later become vital in her own career.

One close family friend recalls how Susie handled these challenges with a maturity that belied her age. "She wasn't one to dwell on things or ask for sympathy. She'd face what was in front of her and move forward, just like her father taught her. It's no surprise she ended up where she did," they said.

After high school, Susie decided to pursue a degree in English, a choice that some found curious given her father's athletic background. But for Susie, studying English was more than an academic pursuit; it was a way to hone her understanding of language and communication, skills she instinctively knew would be invaluable. Throughout her college years, she explored various ways that language could influence and shape thought, a theme that would later become central to her work in politics.

By the time she graduated, Susie had developed a set of skills that combined her family's values with her own intellectual curiosity. She knew how to observe, to listen, and, above all, to remain resilient in the face of change. These qualities would become the foundation of her career, guiding her through the complex, and often contentious, world of American politics.

Her father's words continued to echo in her mind as she stepped into the professional world. "You don't have to be the loudest voice to be heard," he once told her, a piece of advice she took to heart. Susie knew she was ready to make an impact—not by seeking attention, but by quietly building a legacy of her own.

## Chapter 2: Breaking into Politics

Susie Wiles's entry into politics wasn't part of some grand plan. Instead, it was a series of quiet choices that gradually led her into the arena. Her early roles were less about making a name for herself and more about gaining insight into the rhythms of political life, often from the sidelines. But even then, her colleagues noticed something different about her—something that set her apart from the usual faces eager to climb the political ladder.

Her first official political role came in the late 1970s, when she joined Jack Kemp's team as a staff assistant. Kemp, a former NFL quarterback turned congressman, was a rising star in Republican politics. Known for his engaging personality and forward-thinking ideas, particularly on economic policy, Kemp was one of the few politicians actively working to bridge traditional conservative values with innovative solutions to economic issues. To Susie, he was a figure not unlike her father—a larger-than-life persona but also grounded in purpose and integrity.

Working for Kemp allowed Susie to see the demands of political life up close. Her role was mostly administrative, handling tasks like organizing schedules and liaising with other members of Kemp's team. But she didn't treat it as merely a job. Instead, she watched, listened, and absorbed everything around her, taking note of the ways people communicated, the subtle strategies in positioning and messaging. Kemp's approach to politics was a lesson in itself; he was a proponent of "compassionate conservatism," a philosophy that spoke to Susie's own belief that politics could be a force for positive change.

"Jack wasn't just talking to voters—he was talking with them," Susie would later reflect. "He knew how to connect with people, even when they didn't agree with him."

While many staffers saw the fast pace and intensity of the job as exhausting, Susie found it invigorating. Every day, she observed how policy ideas were crafted, discussed, and, sometimes, transformed to meet political realities. She learned that politics wasn't always about idealism but rather about finding common ground—even if that meant making concessions. Watching Kemp maneuver through these complexities left a deep impression on her.

After a few years with Kemp, Susie was invited to join Ronald Reagan's 1980 presidential campaign as the deputy director of scheduling. For a young woman who had only recently entered politics, it was an incredible opportunity. Reagan's campaign was a behemoth, both in terms of its scale and its ambition.

Susie joined a team that was focused, driven, and deeply committed to Reagan's vision of a more optimistic America. The work was demanding, but Susie quickly proved herself invaluable, coordinating schedules, ensuring that key events ran smoothly, and managing countless details that often went unnoticed by others.

It was here that she began to see the importance of strategy on a larger scale. Running a campaign wasn't just about rallies and speeches; it was about creating a narrative that resonated with voters across different backgrounds and beliefs. Reagan's team excelled at this, turning his personality and principles into a cohesive message that felt both relatable and inspiring. Susie, though not yet in a position to shape this message, was deeply inspired by it. She saw how a well-crafted narrative could capture hearts and minds, something that would shape her own approach to political strategy in the years to come.

"Reagan's campaign was like an orchestra, and everyone had their role to play," Susie once said to a friend. "But it was the conductor—Reagan himself—who gave us all a sense of direction. He knew what he stood for, and people felt that."

During this time, Susie's ability to anticipate needs and stay calm under pressure began to stand out. Her knack for handling complex situations with a quiet determination caught the attention of senior staff. Unlike others who sought recognition, Susie remained content with doing her work well, even if it meant going unnoticed. To her, the satisfaction came from knowing that the job was done right and that she had contributed to something bigger than herself.

One campaign member recalled an incident in which an event nearly went off the rails due to a scheduling conflict. While others panicked, Susie calmly assessed the situation, found an alternative, and ensured that the event went on without a hitch. "She didn't need praise or thanks," he said. "She just got it done. That's the kind of person you want on your team."

The success of Reagan's campaign and his subsequent election as President cemented Susie's belief that she was in the right field. But it also opened her eyes to the broader possibilities within politics. Working on a presidential campaign had been exhilarating, but she realized that her true passion lay in the art of strategy itself. It wasn't enough for her to be part of the background; she wanted to understand how decisions were made, how narratives were crafted, and how strategies could be adapted to influence public opinion.

In the early 1980s, Susie continued to work within the political sphere, now with a sharpened focus on strategy and decision-making. Her role in the Executive Office of the President allowed her to observe the inner workings of the White House, further shaping her understanding of the political landscape. Here, she witnessed how policies were crafted and implemented, how public opinion was measured, and how communication strategies were tailored to align with the administration's goals. She saw firsthand the balancing act between staying true to one's principles and responding to the demands of the public.

For Susie, these experiences weren't just about learning the mechanics of politics; they were about understanding the psychology behind it. She became increasingly interested in how people's beliefs and values could be influenced by carefully crafted messages. She saw that politics was as much about perception as it was about policy, a realization that would define her career.

By the time she left the Reagan administration, Susie had developed a clear sense of direction. She no longer saw herself as merely an assistant or a scheduler; she was a strategist in the making, someone who understood that true power often lay behind the scenes. It was this realization that set her on a path that would eventually lead her to become one of the most influential figures in American political strategy.

In the years that followed, Susie's journey would take her from state politics in Florida to national campaigns, but the lessons she learned during her early years remained with her. The quiet determination she had developed, combined with her growing expertise in strategic communication, positioned her as a trusted and formidable operative. She had seen the machinery of politics from the inside, and she knew that her path would be one of influence, even if it meant staying out of the spotlight.

# Chapter 3: Navigating the Local Arena

After her time in the Reagan administration, Susie Wiles returned to her home state of Florida, where she would begin one of the most formative chapters of her career. Entering the realm of state and local politics might have seemed like a step down after working on a presidential campaign, but Susie understood that real change often happened closer to home. State and local governments were the front lines where policies directly impacted people's daily lives, and it was here that Susie saw an opportunity to use her talents in strategy and organization to make a tangible difference.

In the early 1990s, Susie accepted a role that would become pivotal to her growth as a political strategist: Chief of Staff to Jacksonville's Mayor John Delaney. Delaney, a practical, results-oriented leader, shared Susie's passion for public service and dedication to efficient governance. They formed a close working relationship built on trust, shared values, and a commitment to the city's progress. As Chief of Staff, Susie was responsible for coordinating city operations, managing the mayor's office, and ensuring that Delaney's agenda was effectively communicated and executed.

One of her former colleagues recalls, "Susie had this calm, collected way of working. No matter how chaotic things got, she was the one keeping everything on track. She never let the pressure show. She'd just look at you and say, 'Alright, let's figure it out,' and somehow, you'd feel like everything was going to be fine."

Jacksonville at the time was a city in transition. It was grappling with the challenges of rapid growth, economic shifts, and the need to modernize its infrastructure. The mayor's office faced mounting pressures from various interest groups, each with its own demands and priorities. In this environment, Susie's ability to listen, negotiate, and build consensus became invaluable. She was more than just an organizer; she was a bridge-builder, someone who could bring together opposing voices and find a path forward that balanced competing interests.

One of her first major challenges came during Delaney's ambitious plan to revitalize the downtown area, a project that required careful coordination among city officials, business leaders, and community organizations. The plan was met with skepticism, especially from residents who were concerned about the costs and potential disruptions. Susie knew that success would depend not only on clear communication but also on addressing the community's concerns with transparency and respect.

In a series of public meetings, Susie worked tirelessly behind the scenes, preparing Delaney and his team to address the public's questions and concerns. She understood that people wanted to be heard, and she ensured that the city's approach was inclusive. Under her guidance, the administration adopted a more open communication strategy, holding regular town halls and releasing detailed updates on the project's progress and budget. Her approach won over many skeptics, and by the time the project was completed, the downtown area had undergone a transformation that not only improved the city's economic prospects but also strengthened community ties.

"She had this ability to see the big picture and the little details at the same time," a former city council member noted. "Most people focus on one or the other, but Susie managed both. She'd be thinking about the end goal but also making sure each step was handled just right. It was impressive."

In her role, Susie also tackled several issues that required political deftness and a steady hand. Budget negotiations were particularly challenging, as they often involved intense back-and-forth with council members who had their own ideas about spending priorities. Susie's approach was one of quiet persuasion; she didn't strong-arm her way through disagreements. Instead, she listened carefully, found common ground, and presented solutions that appealed to both sides of the debate. This earned her respect not only from her colleagues in the mayor's office but also from council members and community leaders who valued her fair-minded approach.

One of the key accomplishments during this time was the River City Renaissance project, a multi-million dollar initiative aimed at revitalizing Jacksonville's riverfront and historic neighborhoods. This project required significant public and private investment, as well as navigating environmental regulations and logistical hurdles. As Chief of Staff, Susie played a crucial role in coordinating efforts between the city, developers, and state agencies to ensure the project's success.

Susie's ability to handle complex, multi-layered projects with grace and determination did not go unnoticed. Her work on the River City Renaissance project earned praise from local media, which highlighted her role in bridging gaps between the city's administration and the various stakeholders involved. While she rarely sought the spotlight, her reputation as an effective leader grew steadily. Jacksonville residents began to see her as a steady hand within city government, someone who was deeply committed to the community's progress.

Beyond her official duties, Susie also took a keen interest in mentoring younger staff members in the mayor's office. She believed that a strong team was essential to achieving long-term success, and she took time to share her experiences and insights with those around her. Many of her former colleagues credit her with instilling in them a sense of dedication and professionalism that has shaped their own careers.

One former staff member recalls, "Susie wasn't just a boss. She was a mentor. She'd take time to explain why a decision was made, not just tell us what to do. That made all the difference. We didn't just feel like employees; we felt like part of something bigger."

Her time as Chief of Staff also deepened her understanding of the intricacies of state and local politics. Unlike national campaigns, which often hinge on broad narratives and large-scale media outreach, local politics required a different approach. Here, relationships mattered more than soundbites, and trust was built one conversation at a time. Susie learned that small gestures—listening to a concerned resident, following up on a promise, or acknowledging someone's effort—could go a long way in building goodwill and fostering a sense of community.

As the years went by, Susie's influence in Jacksonville grew, and so did her skills as a strategist. She became known for her ability to balance competing priorities without compromising on her principles. Whether it was negotiating budget cuts, working with neighborhood leaders to address community needs, or coordinating responses to unexpected crises, Susie approached each challenge with a calm, methodical mindset that kept the city on course.

Her work during this period would lay the foundation for her later success on the national stage. The skills she honed in Jacksonville—the ability to manage complex projects, build consensus, and navigate political tensions—would serve her well in the years to come. But beyond the technical skills, it was her dedication to public service and her belief in the power of thoughtful, strategic leadership that defined her time in local politics.

Reflecting on her experience years later, Susie described it as one of the most rewarding times of her life. "There's something special about local government," she said in an interview. "You see the impact of your work up close, and you get to know the people you're serving. It's not just policy—it's personal."

As she prepared to take her next steps, Susie knew that her time in Jacksonville had given her a unique perspective on the challenges and opportunities in American politics. She had seen what could be accomplished when people worked together with a shared sense of purpose, and she carried this vision with her as she moved into new roles. Her journey through state and local politics was complete, but the lessons she had learned would remain with her, guiding her decisions and shaping her approach to the complex world of national strategy that awaited her.

# Chapter 4: The 2010 Florida Gubernatorial Campaign

In 2010, the Florida gubernatorial race was set to be one of the most competitive in the country, with stakes that reached far beyond the state. The Republican primary alone had attracted intense attention, as Rick Scott, a relatively unknown businessman with no political experience, had entered the race against Bill McCollum, a seasoned politician and then Florida's Attorney General. At the time, Scott was an outsider—an underdog with significant financial resources but no real foothold in the state's political sphere. To secure a victory, he needed a campaign team that could break through the noise, strategically position him, and build a connection with voters skeptical of his outsider status. Enter Susie Wiles.

Susie joined Scott's team as the campaign manager, and from the outset, it was clear she would need to approach this race differently than any before. The political climate was turbulent, with an electorate deeply concerned about the economy, healthcare, and transparency in government. Scott's background in healthcare, specifically his tenure as CEO of the hospital chain Columbia/HCA, was both an asset and a potential liability; the company had faced a major fraud investigation, resulting in a historic settlement.

Susie knew they would need to address this issue head-on, framing Scott as someone who had learned from his experiences and was focused on bringing business acumen to Florida's government.

"People are going to talk about the past," she told the team early on. "But we're going to remind them that Rick's here to create a future."

From day one, Susie's strategy focused on differentiating Scott from career politicians. She framed him as a no-nonsense, results-oriented businessman who was ready to take on the political establishment. But it wasn't just about messaging; Susie knew that to reach Florida's diverse electorate, they would need a grassroots approach. She organized a series of town hall meetings, campaign stops, and media appearances that emphasized Scott's commitment to hearing directly from the voters. The campaign became one of connection and engagement, designed to build trust and counteract any negative perceptions associated with his business background.

A key component of Susie's strategy was transparency. She believed that Scott's past wouldn't be a hurdle as long as they addressed it openly. During public events, Scott often spoke candidly about his experiences in the healthcare industry, framing them as lessons learned. Susie ensured that these moments were highlighted, showcasing a side of Scott that was open and, perhaps unexpectedly, relatable. This approach resonated with voters who were looking for authenticity, and it set Scott apart from his opponent, who had decades of political experience but was seen as part of the establishment.

"Rick isn't a politician, and that's his strength," she explained in one campaign meeting. "People are tired of the same old rhetoric. They want someone who understands the real world, who's had successes and setbacks, and who isn't afraid to talk about them."

Susie's approach worked. Scott's outsider status, initially seen as a disadvantage, became the very thing that propelled him forward. In a primary race that was anticipated to be an uphill battle, Scott surged ahead. As Election Day approached, Scott's campaign was gaining momentum, and the polls showed a tight race. Susie's strategy had managed to turn Scott's perceived weaknesses into assets, and the focus on transparency and economic reform resonated deeply with voters facing financial hardships.

The victory in the primary was a defining moment for both Scott and Susie. But the real challenge was still ahead: the general election. Scott would be facing Democrat Alex Sink, Florida's Chief Financial Officer, in what was shaping up to be one of the closest races in the state's history. With the eyes of the nation on Florida, Susie knew they needed to elevate their game.

The general election campaign became a marathon of messaging, outreach, and relentless media strategy. Susie expanded the team's focus, integrating digital advertising, targeted mail campaigns, and televised debates. She worked closely with Scott to sharpen his message, focusing on job creation, economic growth, and government accountability—issues that resonated strongly with Floridians. Each campaign appearance was meticulously planned, with Susie overseeing even the smallest details to ensure the message remained consistent and compelling.

One of the most critical moments of the campaign came during the televised debates. Scott, known more for his business background than his public speaking skills, had to connect with voters in a way that felt personal and genuine. Susie prepared him rigorously, running through potential questions and helping him craft responses that were both direct and empathetic. Her emphasis was on showing Scott's human side, something that had often been overshadowed by his intense focus on business and results.

"We don't need Rick to be a polished politician," she reminded the team. "We need him to be real. Voters want to know that he understands their struggles."

The debates were a success, with Scott presenting himself as a practical, solutions-oriented candidate who was willing to take on tough issues. Susie's strategy of focusing on Scott's strengths—his business background, his understanding of job creation, and his commitment to accountability—paid off. As Election Day drew near, polls indicated a dead heat, but Susie remained optimistic. She knew they had done everything possible to communicate Scott's vision and connect with voters.

The night of the election was tense. As results began to come in, it became clear that the race was closer than anyone had anticipated. By the early hours of the morning, Scott had emerged victorious, winning by a margin so narrow that it underscored just how crucial every aspect of Susie's campaign strategy had been. For her, the victory wasn't just a political win; it was a testament to the power of strategy, authenticity, and the ability to adapt in the face of challenges.

Scott's victory in the 2010 gubernatorial race was a watershed moment for Susie. She had not only managed a challenging campaign but had also solidified her reputation as one of Florida's top political strategists. The lessons she learned during this campaign would go on to shape her approach in future roles, reinforcing her belief in the importance of transparency, resilience, and staying true to one's strengths.

Reflecting on the campaign years later, a colleague said, "Susie has this incredible ability to see potential in situations that others might overlook. She took what seemed like a weakness and turned it into Rick's biggest asset. That's her gift—she knows how to connect with people's real concerns and turn them into something positive."

In the years that followed, Susie's work on the 2010 campaign would continue to be studied as a masterclass in political strategy. For her, though, the victory was less about personal accolades and more about the satisfaction of helping an outsider break through. She had helped Rick Scott navigate the complexities of a high-stakes race and emerge as Florida's governor, a role that would come to define both his career and hers.

As Susie looked forward to new challenges, she carried with her the lessons from this pivotal campaign. She had learned the value of staying grounded, of embracing transparency, and of trusting her instincts. These principles would guide her as she took on future campaigns, each one an opportunity to refine her skills and make an impact. For Susie Wiles, the 2010 Florida gubernatorial race wasn't just a chapter in her career; it was a defining moment that underscored her dedication to public service and her belief in the transformative power of strategic, compassionate leadership.

# Chapter 5: Joining Trump's 2016 Campaign

When Susie Wiles joined Donald Trump's 2016 presidential campaign, the decision raised eyebrows across Florida's political landscape. She had already established herself as a skilled strategist with a history of helping unconventional candidates find success, yet this campaign was unlike any she had taken on before. The Trump campaign was divisive, polarizing, and unpredictable, with a message and a candidate who broke nearly every political norm. For Susie, it was an opportunity to apply her strategic talents on a national stage while representing her home state, Florida—a crucial battleground that could tip the election in Trump's favor.

Her arrival on the campaign was not a result of traditional recruitment. Trump's team sought her out specifically for her deep understanding of Florida's political terrain and her proven track record. In political circles, Florida is known for its unique mix of voter demographics: the retirees, the Latino communities, the suburban families, and the young professionals in cities like Orlando and Miami. It's a state where no one group's support is guaranteed, and winning requires a strategy that acknowledges Florida's diversity. Susie knew this well, and it became clear that she would play a key role in helping Trump secure the state.

"Florida isn't just one state," she told campaign staff during her first meeting. "It's multiple regions, each with its own identity and concerns. You don't just win Florida—you win Miami-Dade, the I-4 corridor, the Panhandle. Each one needs its own approach."

Susie was no stranger to complex political dynamics, but she quickly recognized that this campaign would present new challenges. Trump's approach to politics was direct and often controversial, appealing to voters frustrated with the status quo but alienating others who found his style too brash. Susie understood that while Trump's message resonated strongly with certain voter groups, there was also a need to bridge gaps and present a message that appealed across the board. Her first step was to assess the strengths and weaknesses of the campaign's current efforts in Florida and identify areas where her experience could make a difference.

One of Susie's first moves was to expand outreach efforts in traditionally underserved areas, particularly within Latino communities. Trump's stance on immigration had caused significant backlash among Latino voters, and Susie knew they needed to address these concerns if they wanted to gain ground. She organized a series of community events focused on topics that mattered most to these voters—economic opportunities, job growth, and support for small businesses. The messaging was careful and specific, emphasizing Trump's plans for economic revitalization and safety without directly wading into more contentious topics.

"You can't go in with a one-size-fits-all message," she reminded the team during strategy sessions. "People need to feel that we understand their specific issues, that we're not just asking for their vote but listening to what they need."

The Florida team also increased its focus on voter registration efforts, particularly in the I-4 corridor, a critical swing area stretching from Tampa to Daytona Beach. This region, with its mix of urban and suburban communities, has often been a deciding factor in statewide elections. Susie's goal was simple: to drive up turnout in areas that leaned Republican while appealing to undecided voters who felt disconnected from both parties. She emphasized the importance of a robust ground game, organizing volunteers to knock on doors, hold neighborhood events, and communicate directly with voters. Her approach was a return to grassroots campaigning—a method she believed was especially effective in a state as diverse as Florida.

One senior campaign member later noted, "Susie has this instinct for understanding people's concerns. She doesn't just see numbers or demographics; she sees individuals, each with their own reasons for voting. That's why she's so effective."

As the election drew closer, Susie's efforts intensified. She worked closely with Trump's communications team to tailor messaging specifically for Florida, focusing on economic issues, job creation, and a commitment to veterans—issues that resonated particularly well with the state's large retiree population and military families. She also coordinated a series of appearances and rallies, each carefully planned to maximize impact in key regions. Every detail mattered, from the timing of the events to the locations, ensuring that Trump's message reached as many voters as possible.

One of her most effective strategies was to lean into the frustration many Floridians felt toward Washington's political elite. Trump's brand as an outsider resonated with those who felt their voices were overlooked, and Susie crafted messaging that reinforced this sentiment. She helped shape Trump's speeches in Florida, encouraging him to speak directly to these frustrations and position himself as a solution to the government disconnect. This approach resonated particularly well in the Panhandle and other conservative-leaning areas, where voters were eager for a candidate who promised a fresh start.

"Susie understood Florida better than most," recalled a campaign volunteer. "She knew what people were fed up with, and she knew how to make them feel heard. That's not something you can fake; it's knowing the people you're talking to."

Despite her strategic brilliance, the campaign was not without its obstacles. Media coverage of Trump's comments and policies sometimes created new challenges, and Susie had to constantly adapt her approach to keep the campaign focused and united. In the face of controversy, she kept the team grounded, focusing on the goal rather than getting caught up in distractions. Her steady hand during turbulent moments became a source of confidence for the Florida team, who looked to her for guidance when the national campaign faced criticism.

By the time Election Day arrived, Susie's efforts had transformed Florida into a tightly contested battleground where Trump held a significant edge. Her meticulous attention to voter outreach, tailored messaging, and strategic event planning had paid off. As the results rolled in, it became clear that Florida would be one of the deciding states in the election— and it was leaning in Trump's favor.

When the final results were announced, Trump had won Florida by a narrow margin, securing a vital 29 electoral votes. It was a victory that stunned many and underscored the effectiveness of Susie's strategy. Her work in Florida had not only helped deliver the state for Trump but had also cemented her reputation as a top-tier strategist capable of navigating complex political landscapes and turning challenges into advantages.

In the aftermath of the election, political analysts and insiders acknowledged the pivotal role Susie had played. Florida had been a must-win state, and her ability to connect with diverse voter groups, anticipate challenges, and adapt to an ever-evolving campaign environment was crucial to the outcome. Susie's success wasn't just in the win itself but in how she had orchestrated it, balancing the candidate's bold personality with the nuanced messaging needed to reach Florida's diverse electorate.

Reflecting on the experience, Susie remained characteristically humble. For her, the campaign wasn't about her own reputation or personal accolades; it was about seeing a vision through, achieving the impossible by leveraging the power of connection and strategic communication.

Years later, one of her closest colleagues would sum up her contribution this way: "Susie wasn't just a strategist—she was the reason we believed we could win Florida. She saw the state not as a map of voting districts but as a community of people with real concerns. That's why she succeeded, and that's why she's one of the best."

The 2016 campaign became a defining chapter in Susie Wiles's career, one that would leave an indelible mark on Florida's political history. Her work on Trump's campaign showcased her ability to adapt to unconventional circumstances, her understanding of grassroots mobilization, and her commitment to a well-crafted strategy. As she looked ahead to future roles, she carried with her the lessons of 2016—a testament to the power of strategic foresight, empathy, and resilience in the face of extraordinary challenges.

# Chapter 6: The 2020 Re-Election Battle

In 2020, Susie Wiles found herself once again at the center of a presidential campaign. This time, it wasn't just about strategizing for an outsider candidate but defending the incumbent president's record amidst a profoundly divided nation. Donald Trump's re-election campaign carried high stakes, especially in battleground states like Florida, where Susie's expertise had proven essential in the 2016 victory. She returned to the campaign with a well-earned reputation as one of the Republican Party's most skilled strategists, and her mission was clear: to secure Florida for Trump once more.

The political climate in 2020 was starkly different from four years prior. A global pandemic had reshaped everyday life, racial justice protests had brought social issues to the forefront, and partisan divides were at an all-time high. In Florida, these divisions ran deep, with communities polarized over issues of health, economy, and civil rights. Susie understood that winning Florida required not only strategic messaging but also a deep understanding of the issues that mattered most to Floridians—and how they had shifted since Trump's first campaign.

From the start, Susie recognized that 2020's campaign wouldn't succeed with a one-size-fits-all approach. Each region of Florida had unique concerns, and the pandemic amplified this reality. In the early days of the campaign, she held strategy meetings with staff and local advisors to assess how the pandemic was affecting different parts of the state, from Miami's tourism-dependent economy to the agricultural communities in Central Florida and the retirement enclaves along the coast.

"Look, we can't approach this like it's 2016," she told her team during an initial meeting. "People's lives have changed. They're worried about their health, their jobs, their families. We need to speak to those worries and offer solutions."

Susie's strategy hinged on three pillars: economic recovery, public safety, and community engagement. She pushed for a grassroots campaign that emphasized direct voter outreach and tailored messaging that acknowledged the specific challenges facing each community. To adapt to the pandemic's constraints, her team launched a robust digital campaign, targeting Florida's diverse electorate through social media, email newsletters, and virtual town halls. She made sure that every message conveyed empathy, understanding, and the promise of a return to stability.

One area where Susie's efforts were particularly focused was Florida's senior population, a demographic that had largely supported Trump in 2016 but now faced unique concerns due to COVID-19. Seniors were worried about health risks, vaccine availability, and the economic impact on their retirement plans. Susie arranged virtual events specifically for senior voters, where campaign representatives addressed these issues and provided updates on the administration's efforts to protect them. She also advocated for clear communication around Trump's healthcare policies, recognizing that access to healthcare had become a top priority for many seniors.

Another challenge was the shifting political landscape among Latino voters, who represented a significant portion of Florida's electorate. Unlike in 2016, the Latino community in 2020 was far from monolithic, with various groups expressing differing concerns over immigration, economic recovery, and social policies. Susie knew they had to approach each community with a unique strategy. She worked closely with local leaders in Miami-Dade to craft a message that resonated with Cuban American voters, emphasizing anti-socialist rhetoric and economic freedom. Meanwhile, in areas with larger Puerto Rican populations, she focused on recovery efforts following Hurricane Maria and the administration's response to the pandemic.

"Floridians are diverse, and that's our strength," she told her team. "But if we don't respect that diversity in our messaging, we're going to lose people. Every vote counts, and every community needs to know that we hear them."

Susie's understanding of Florida's demographic complexities allowed the campaign to remain competitive in a state where the electorate was increasingly fragmented. But her role wasn't just about crafting messages; it was also about keeping the team focused amid the turmoil. The 2020 campaign was often chaotic, with frequent shifts in national strategy, intense media scrutiny, and controversies that sometimes overshadowed the campaign's core messages. Susie became known as a steadying presence, someone who kept her team grounded even when headlines and social media chatter threatened to derail their focus.

One team member recalls, "Susie was always the calm in the storm. When things got tense, she'd say, 'Focus on the people we're serving. Let's control what we can control.' She reminded us why we were there and kept us looking forward."

Her pragmatic approach proved crucial as Election Day approached and Florida's polling remained tight. Susie doubled down on community engagement, urging her team to ramp up door-to-door outreach where possible, following safety protocols to reassure voters. The digital outreach also intensified, with targeted ads, virtual rallies, and a significant investment in Spanish-language media. Susie knew that every interaction, no matter how small, could be the difference between a win and a loss in Florida's razor-thin margins.

On the night of the election, the atmosphere in the campaign headquarters was charged with anticipation. As results trickled in, Florida became one of the first major battleground states to report, and it quickly became clear that Trump had secured the state. The win was a testament to Susie's strategy and her ability to mobilize a deeply divided electorate in one of the most contentious elections in recent history. Though Trump ultimately lost the national election, Florida's results were a bright spot for the campaign and a reminder of the pivotal role Susie had played in one of the nation's most critical battlegrounds.

In the aftermath, analysts pointed to Florida as a case study in effective, tailored campaigning amidst unprecedented challenges. Susie's work on the 2020 campaign was lauded by colleagues and political commentators alike, who noted her ability to balance empathy with strategic foresight. For Susie, the experience was both challenging and reaffirming, underscoring her belief that successful campaigns aren't just about winning votes—they're about connecting with people on a human level, understanding their lives, and offering a vision they can believe in.

Reflecting on the campaign, Susie said, "2020 showed us how resilient people are. It was a tough year, and a tough campaign, but what kept us going was knowing that we were representing people's voices. That's what politics should be about—serving people and addressing what matters to them."

Her work in 2020 left an indelible mark not only on Florida politics but also on her legacy as a strategist. She had navigated one of the most complex elections in modern history, bringing experience, empathy, and clarity to an otherwise turbulent race. As she looked to the future, Susie knew that the lessons of 2020 would stay with her, guiding her approach to public service and political strategy in the years to come. Her role in Trump's re-election battle was yet another testament to her unwavering commitment to thoughtful, people-centered politics—an approach that had come to define her career and would continue to shape her path forward.

# Chapter 7: Power and Controversy

As Susie Wiles's career evolved, so too did the influence she wielded behind the scenes in American politics. She became known not just as a strategist but as a power broker—someone who operated in the quiet shadows of campaigns and policy decisions, rarely seen but deeply felt. With her rise came inevitable scrutiny, as journalists and political observers began to ask questions about her connections, her influence, and the methods she employed to achieve her goals. Wiles was no stranger to controversy, nor was she intimidated by it. In a field that often blurred the lines between loyalty and opportunism, her dedication to her candidates and causes was both her greatest strength and a point of contention.

Wiles's connections were vast, stretching across political landscapes, party lines, and interest groups. Those close to her often remarked on her ability to build and maintain relationships with key figures, regardless of ideology or party affiliation. This network was one of her greatest assets. It enabled her to tap into insights from a wide range of perspectives, often giving her a clearer picture of the political terrain than others might have. Yet, to her critics, this network sometimes appeared as evidence of an agenda that went beyond her role as a strategist. Susie's access to top-level information, coupled with her skill in navigating political sensitivities, gave her a reputation as someone who could be either a valuable ally or a formidable opponent.

"Susie knows everyone, and I mean everyone," one longtime political observer commented. "It's hard to find anyone in Florida politics, and even beyond, who hasn't worked with her, crossed paths with her, or heard of her. Her network is a quiet kind of power, and it's probably her most valuable asset."

One of the most discussed aspects of her career was her involvement in the campaigns of high-profile, sometimes divisive candidates. Critics argued that her support for figures like Rick Scott and Donald Trump indicated a willingness to align herself with candidates whose policies and views attracted significant opposition. However, those who worked closely with her offered a different perspective. To them, Susie's focus was less about ideology and more about strategy. Her goal was to see the success of her candidate, whatever the cause might be. She saw herself not as a promoter of any specific agenda but as a professional committed to the art and science of campaigning.

"Susie doesn't pick sides based on ideology. She's focused on the work—on winning," a former colleague explained. "She's a strategist first and foremost, and she does what she believes will serve the campaign best. She's not interested in being a cheerleader. She's interested in results."

However, her role often meant navigating controversies that could have unraveled a lesser strategist's career. One such controversy arose during Rick Scott's gubernatorial campaign, where she faced questions regarding her handling of his background in the healthcare industry, specifically the Medicare fraud scandal tied to Columbia/HCA, the company Scott had once led. Opponents argued that Wiles downplayed or sidestepped the issue, while her team countered that she had approached it transparently, positioning Scott as a candidate who had learned from past experiences and was ready to lead with accountability.

The accusations did not seem to faze her. In interviews, Susie responded with calm composure, focusing not on the scandal but on Scott's qualifications and vision for Florida. Her approach, some said, was both calculated and effective—she managed to direct attention away from the accusations and toward the policies her candidate intended to implement. The voters ultimately sided with her strategy, and Scott's victory in Florida became a testament to her ability to neutralize potential damage and keep a campaign on course.

As her career progressed, Susie's handling of controversy became more nuanced. By the time she joined Trump's team in 2016, she had learned to manage the dual demands of loyalty and pragmatism, balancing her commitment to her candidates with a clear-eyed view of the political stakes. Trump's campaign, with its polarizing messages and unconventional tactics, was a minefield of controversy from the beginning. For Susie, it was an opportunity to test her skills in an environment where every statement, action, and policy was scrutinized and debated on a national level.

One of the challenges she faced was Trump's outspoken, often controversial rhetoric, which could alienate certain voter groups while rallying others. While she admired his determination and shared his view on many issues, Susie had to work within the campaign to keep its message controlled, at least in Florida. Her approach was to craft messaging that highlighted Trump's policies in terms that spoke directly to Floridians' concerns, focusing on job creation, economic revitalization, and public safety. This tactic allowed her to sidestep some of the more controversial topics that dominated national headlines while ensuring that her candidate's strengths were front and center in Florida.

"Susie knew how to make the message palatable without diluting it," recalled a member of the Trump campaign. "She has this way of focusing on the positives, on what's relevant to the voter. She doesn't ignore the challenges, but she finds a way to frame them in a way that works."

Despite her ability to navigate controversy skillfully, Susie wasn't immune to criticism. Some political analysts suggested that her approach of focusing on strategic gains sometimes came at the expense of transparency. They argued that while she excelled in sidestepping scandals, her reluctance to confront them directly could create an impression of evasion. In response, her supporters pointed out that Susie's role as a strategist was not to defend every aspect of her candidate's record but to keep the campaign focused on its goals.

"Susie isn't here to fight battles in the press," said a former colleague. "She's here to win elections. And that's what makes her one of the best in the business."

The controversies she faced weren't confined to her candidates. As her influence grew, Susie herself became a target for criticism, especially from those who viewed her as emblematic of the blurred lines between politics and influence. Her network of connections, which spanned politicians, lobbyists, and business leaders, became a focal point for those questioning the role of strategists in shaping policy and public opinion. The suggestion was that her influence went beyond campaign management—that she held a sway over political decisions that extended into policy-making. Some critics saw her as part of a larger problem in American politics, where unelected strategists could wield significant power without accountability to the public.

However, for Susie, these criticisms were merely part of the territory. She rarely responded to personal attacks, instead letting her work speak for itself. To her, the controversies and critiques were a natural consequence of her position; they came with the responsibility of being a trusted advisor in high-stakes environments. Those close to her knew that she was driven not by personal ambition but by a commitment to her work and the candidates she chose to support.

In the end, the controversies surrounding Susie Wiles have only added to her mystique. To her critics, she remains an enigmatic figure who operates in the shadows of power, influencing outcomes without stepping into the limelight. To her allies, she is a master strategist—a professional who brings clarity and direction to campaigns, even in the most challenging and divisive climates. For Susie, the truth likely lies somewhere in between. She is a woman of contradictions, both deeply committed and unapologetically pragmatic, a strategist who knows that success in politics is often less about ideals and more about execution.

Her career thus far has been one of balancing power and controversy, influence and discretion. And for Susie Wiles, that balance is precisely what defines her work. She operates with a steadfast belief in the power of strategy and the art of persuasion, even as she navigates the inevitable controversies that come with wielding influence behind the scenes. In a world where politics is rarely straightforward, Susie remains focused on her mission, understanding that every campaign, every controversy, is simply another challenge to be managed.

# Chapter 8: The Split with DeSantis

Susie Wiles's career has been marked by strategic alliances with some of the most influential figures in politics, but few relationships were as intriguing—or as publicly scrutinized—as her partnership with Florida Governor Ron DeSantis. This relationship, which began with mutual respect and collaboration, ultimately unraveled in a high-profile split that left many political insiders wondering what had gone wrong. The end of Susie's professional alliance with DeSantis marked a pivotal point in her career, one that revealed both the complexities of political loyalty and the often fragile nature of alliances in a field where ambition and power intertwine.

When Susie first joined DeSantis's team during his 2018 gubernatorial campaign, it seemed like a natural fit. DeSantis, a relatively unknown congressman at the time, needed someone with deep knowledge of Florida's political landscape and the experience to guide him through a challenging race. Susie, with her formidable network and a reputation as one of Florida's top political strategists, was the ideal candidate. DeSantis's team recognized her ability to turn a campaign into a finely tuned operation, and Susie saw in DeSantis a candidate with potential, someone who could carry Florida's conservative agenda forward.

Her role in the 2018 campaign was instrumental. From the beginning, Susie crafted a strategy that highlighted DeSantis's support for President Trump, a move that resonated deeply with Florida's conservative voters. She understood that aligning DeSantis with Trump's base would not only set him apart from his competitors but also energize a loyal voter demographic. It was a calculated decision, one that positioned DeSantis as a defender of Trump's policies at a time when such an endorsement was particularly influential in Florida.

"DeSantis needed credibility with the Trump voters," one campaign staffer noted. "Susie knew that Florida's conservatives were looking for someone who would champion their values, and she leaned into that connection with Trump. It was a bold move, but it worked."

The campaign strategy Susie devised was a masterclass in targeted messaging and voter mobilization. She organized rallies, honed DeSantis's talking points, and oversaw outreach efforts that reached every corner of Florida. Her approach was thorough and relentless. She knew that to win, DeSantis needed to establish himself not just as a conservative but as a candidate who understood Florida's diverse voter landscape. By Election Day,

DeSantis had gained significant traction, securing a narrow but decisive victory that would elevate him from relative obscurity to the governorship. And while DeSantis emerged as a rising star in Republican politics, Susie's role in his success was unmistakable.

However, as DeSantis took office, the dynamics of their relationship began to shift. Susie had entered the campaign with a clear understanding of her role: she was there to help win the election. But once the campaign was over, DeSantis's circle began to shrink, and he appeared to surround himself with advisors who were loyal to him personally, rather than loyal to the campaign or its strategic objectives. Susie found herself increasingly distanced from decision-making, her insights seemingly less valued as DeSantis sought to assert his independence.

The turning point came as DeSantis's team started to diverge on key issues, including communication strategy and policy direction. Susie, a seasoned advisor known for her pragmatic approach, offered guidance based on her understanding of Florida's electorate and her experience managing high-stakes campaigns. But her advice was not always heeded, and as tensions grew, her role became more symbolic than substantive. In private, Susie voiced her concerns, but DeSantis appeared more intent on establishing a brand that was uniquely his own, one that didn't rely on the counsel of his former campaign manager.

This shift was not without precedent. In politics, it's common for elected officials to reshape their inner circles once in office, prioritizing loyalty over strategy. But for Susie, the split was particularly poignant. She had invested deeply in DeSantis's campaign, believing that her role extended beyond winning an election to shaping a vision for Florida's future. Watching from the sidelines as her influence faded, Susie saw a version of DeSantis that was different from the candidate she had helped elect—a governor whose ambitions were growing beyond Florida and whose priorities were increasingly national.

"Once Ron became governor, everything changed," remarked a close associate of Susie's. "She wanted to build something lasting, but it felt like he was focused on his own trajectory, not necessarily the state's long-term needs. There was a disconnect, and Susie wasn't about to play a background role if her input wasn't respected."

The final rupture in their relationship was both sudden and public. As DeSantis's administration took shape, Susie's absence from his advisory team became glaringly obvious to insiders. Speculation swirled about the reasons for her departure, with rumors suggesting everything from ideological differences to personal disputes. Though neither Susie nor DeSantis publicly commented on the split, the implications were clear: her once-critical role in his political rise had come to an abrupt end.

For Susie, the split was a professional setback, but it was also a moment of reflection. Her career had always been defined by her loyalty to the campaigns she worked on, and her willingness to stand behind her candidates even through difficult moments. But this time was different. The end of her relationship with DeSantis underscored a reality she had come to accept—that loyalty in politics is often transactional, and that the alliances forged during campaigns may not withstand the pressures of governance.

Despite the disappointment, Susie did not linger on the fallout. She continued her work, shifting her focus to new opportunities and candidates who valued her approach and experience. Her departure from DeSantis's team did not diminish her standing as a top strategist; if anything, it reinforced her reputation as someone who was unafraid to walk away from alliances that no longer served her vision or her values. For Susie, the experience was a reminder that political loyalty has limits and that her career was built on principles that extended beyond any one candidate.

Years later, as DeSantis's career continued to evolve and his national ambitions became more apparent, observers often looked back on the split with Susie as a defining moment in his trajectory. Some argued that her departure represented a loss of strategic insight, while others saw it as a necessary move for DeSantis to establish his own political identity. For Susie, however, the split was simply another chapter in her career—a moment that revealed the complexities of political alliances and the importance of staying true to one's own approach, even when it meant parting ways with a former ally.

Reflecting on her time with DeSantis, Susie offered a perspective that spoke to her pragmatism and resilience. "Politics isn't about holding on to the past," she once remarked to a friend. "It's about knowing when to step back, when to move forward, and when to let go. I'm proud of what we achieved, but life goes on, and so does the work."

Her departure from DeSantis's team became a symbol of her independence, a testament to her belief in the power of strategy over allegiance. It reminded those around her that Susie Wiles was a strategist who charted her own course, defined not by the candidates she served but by the principles that guided her work. In the world of politics, where loyalty and ambition often clash, Susie's career stood as a reminder that true influence doesn't require proximity to power—it requires integrity, perspective, and a willingness to embrace change.

The split with DeSantis marked the end of one chapter in her career, but it also opened the door to new possibilities. As she continued her work with other candidates and causes, Susie carried with her the lessons of that experience—a recognition of the limits of political loyalty, the value of strategic independence, and the importance of staying true to her own professional identity. For Susie Wiles, the future was always a series of possibilities, each shaped by her commitment to her craft and her vision for the work she believed in.

# Chapter 9: The Return to Trump and 2024

As the 2024 presidential campaign season ramped up, a familiar name returned to Donald Trump's inner circle: Susie Wiles. Known for her sharp political instincts and deep understanding of Florida's political landscape, Susie's comeback was anything but unexpected. In many ways, her re-entry into Trump's orbit underscored her reputation as a "fixer" in high-stakes campaigns—a strategist who knew how to work behind the scenes to keep a candidate's path clear and focused. Her role in Trump's bid for a second term wasn't just a reprise; it was a testament to her expertise and enduring value in an ever-changing political arena.

Susie's renewed involvement in the 2024 campaign was a strategic move by Trump's team. The stakes were higher than ever, and Florida, once again, was a must-win state for Republicans. Trump's team recognized that if there was anyone who could secure the state, it was Susie Wiles. Her insights into Florida's voting patterns, her connections within the state's political infrastructure, and her ability to create tailored messaging for Florida's unique demographic mix positioned her as a key player.

When Susie agreed to join the 2024 campaign, she was clear about her objectives. For her, it wasn't about rehashing the past or relying on the tactics that had worked in 2016. Instead, she approached the campaign with a fresh perspective, understanding that the political climate had changed and that voters were looking for stability and reassurance amidst a turbulent political landscape. She knew that Trump's base remained loyal, but she also recognized the importance of broadening his appeal to reach independents and undecided voters who could tip the scales in crucial swing states.

"2024 isn't 2016 or 2020," she told her team in one of their initial strategy meetings. "We're dealing with a different America—a country that's been through a pandemic, economic uncertainty, and a lot of social change. People want to know what's next. We need to give them a vision that's focused on moving forward, on solving real problems."

One of Susie's first initiatives was to assess the key issues facing voters in Florida and other battleground states. She assembled a team of local experts, data analysts, and field organizers to gather insights directly from the communities. The findings were clear: the economy, public safety, and healthcare remained top concerns, but there was also a rising interest in education policies, infrastructure development, and the cost of living. Floridians, especially, wanted concrete plans that addressed these issues in their daily lives. Susie knew that Trump's messaging would need to evolve to reflect this.

In response, she crafted a strategy that was grounded in specifics, moving away from broad slogans and toward policies that addressed the tangible needs of voters. She emphasized the importance of direct voter outreach, believing that in-person interactions, phone calls, and community events would foster a sense of connection that digital advertising alone could not achieve. Under her guidance, Trump's campaign in Florida launched a series of town hall meetings, small business forums, and community roundtables where local residents could voice their concerns and hear the campaign's solutions.

In these events, Susie encouraged a conversational tone, urging Trump and his surrogates to engage directly with people's questions and to present plans that were both practical and relatable. This approach was particularly effective in suburban and rural areas, where voters appreciated the personal touch and felt their voices were heard. Her strategy focused on creating a campaign that felt accessible, one that didn't talk at voters but rather listened to them.

"People are tired of being talked at," she explained to a group of staffers during a campaign briefing. "They want to feel involved in the conversation, like their input actually matters. We're not here just to give answers; we're here to listen and work with them to find solutions."

A key part of Susie's strategy involved addressing some of the criticisms Trump had faced in previous campaigns. She knew that while his base remained steadfast, there were groups of voters—especially women, suburban families, and young professionals—who felt alienated by his brash style. Her goal was not to change Trump's personality but to create messaging that emphasized his strengths as a leader who cared about American families and their future. She worked closely with the communications team to refine Trump's message, focusing on themes of economic stability, national security, and a renewed commitment to America's middle class.

This time, Susie's role extended beyond Florida. Her influence reached into other battleground states, where her strategies were adapted to local contexts. In Pennsylvania, she focused on job creation and manufacturing, addressing the economic anxieties of working-class voters. In Arizona, she emphasized border security and community safety, two issues that resonated deeply with the state's residents. Her understanding of each state's unique concerns allowed her to tailor Trump's campaign to resonate with a diverse array of voters.

"She has this ability to understand not just what people care about, but why they care about it," noted a senior campaign advisor. "She sees the bigger picture, but she never loses sight of the details that matter to people on the ground."

As the campaign progressed, Susie encountered the familiar challenges of media scrutiny and political opposition. Trump's candidacy continued to polarize the electorate, and his past controversies were frequently highlighted by opponents. Susie responded by reinforcing a disciplined, forward-focused message, urging her team to keep the narrative on the issues rather than engaging in a back-and-forth with critics. She knew that every minute spent defending past controversies was a minute lost to discussing the campaign's future vision.

One of Susie's most effective strategies involved leveraging Trump's rallies as both a show of strength and a platform for policy announcements. Unlike in previous campaigns, where rallies had often focused on energizing the base, Susie saw an opportunity to use these events to unveil detailed plans on key issues. She helped shape Trump's speeches to include specific policy points, turning each rally into a chance to communicate the campaign's roadmap for the next four years.

Through it all, Susie maintained a steady hand, navigating the ebbs and flows of the campaign with a calm resolve that inspired confidence among her team. She understood that the path to victory was not without obstacles, but she was unflinching in her focus on the goal. To her, the 2024 campaign was a culmination of everything she had learned over the years—a test of her ability to adapt, to lead, and to secure a win in the face of unprecedented challenges.

As Election Day approached, Susie's meticulous planning and strategic foresight became evident in the campaign's organization and outreach. Trump's team in Florida was stronger than ever, with an unprecedented level of grassroots support that extended into previously untapped voter segments. Polls indicated a tight race, but Susie was confident in the groundwork they had laid. She had built a campaign that was resilient, adaptable, and attuned to the concerns of everyday Americans.

When the final votes were counted, Trump's performance in Florida was seen as a highlight for the campaign. Although the national results were still being analyzed, Susie's work in Florida—and the influence she had extended to other battleground states—reinforced her status as a master strategist.

Regardless of the final outcome, her role in the 2024 campaign would be remembered as a testament to her expertise, her adaptability, and her deep understanding of American voters.

Reflecting on the campaign, Susie remained pragmatic about her role. "Every election is different," she said to a colleague after the results were announced. "You do your best, you adapt to the circumstances, and you keep moving forward. It's always about the people, about listening to what they need and working to give them a voice. That's what this work is about for me."

Her return to Trump's campaign in 2024 marked both a reunion and a new chapter. It underscored her enduring value in American politics and highlighted the qualities that had defined her career: strategic insight, dedication to the craft, and an unwavering commitment to connecting with voters. As she looked toward the future, Susie knew that her work was far from over. The 2024 campaign had reminded her of the challenges and rewards of her profession, and she remained as committed as ever to the power of thoughtful, people-centered politics.

# Chapter 10: First Woman Chief of Staff

In 2024, Susie Wiles broke new ground when she was appointed as the White House Chief of Staff, making history as the first woman to hold the position. This appointment was not just a milestone for her career; it was a landmark achievement for women in American politics, where the upper echelons of power have long been dominated by men. For Susie, this role was an affirmation of years of dedication, hard work, and a commitment to strategy and excellence. However, with the role came a new set of responsibilities and challenges, ones that would test her resilience, adaptability, and ability to navigate a high-pressure environment that demanded nothing less than her very best.

From the moment the announcement was made, Susie's appointment sparked conversations across the political spectrum. Some celebrated her as a trailblazer, a woman who had earned her place through sheer talent and strategic prowess. Others questioned how her style, honed in the background of campaigns and quiet influence, would translate to the very public and politically charged role of Chief of Staff. The White House Chief of Staff is often seen as the President's closest advisor and gatekeeper, responsible for managing staff, setting priorities, and ensuring the President's agenda is effectively executed. For Susie, it was both an honor and a formidable responsibility.

"It's no small job," she confided to a friend shortly after her appointment. "You don't just oversee policies—you're managing people, handling crises, and making sure the administration runs smoothly. Every decision has weight, and you have to be ready for anything."

Susie entered her new position with a clear sense of purpose. She understood that this role was not about proving herself—she had already done that over decades in political strategy—but about doing the work that needed to be done. Her first step was to evaluate the team around her, assess each department's strengths and weaknesses, and set priorities that aligned with the administration's goals. She knew that efficiency, communication, and cohesion were critical, especially in an environment as fast-paced and high-stakes as the White House.

One of Susie's immediate challenges was establishing a sense of unity within the administration. With different factions representing various interests, ideologies, and policy goals, it was up to her to bring everyone together under a shared mission. This required a delicate balance between respecting the diverse viewpoints within the team and ensuring that the President's agenda remained the guiding force. Susie approached this challenge with her trademark pragmatism, holding one-on-one meetings with senior advisors and department heads to understand their perspectives, address any concerns, and build a foundation of trust.

"Susie has this way of making you feel like your voice matters," said one White House official. "She listens, really listens, and that's not something you find everywhere in politics. She's not just here to manage; she's here to lead."

Her approach quickly gained her respect among her colleagues, who saw in her a leader who valued collaboration over hierarchy. Despite the pressures of the job, she maintained a calm and composed demeanor, even during tense moments. Whether dealing with policy disagreements or urgent crises, Susie's ability to remain steady under pressure became one of her defining traits as Chief of Staff. Her background as a campaign strategist had prepared her well for this aspect of the role; she knew that every challenge was an opportunity to strengthen the administration's focus and resilience.

However, Susie also faced challenges unique to being the first woman in this high-profile position. In meetings with political leaders, media interviews, and public appearances, her every move was scrutinized, sometimes more for her gender than for her expertise. Questions about her leadership style and effectiveness were often framed in ways that her male predecessors had not faced, a reality she was keenly aware of. Susie chose to address these challenges with grace, refusing to let them distract her from her work. To her, the best response was simply to excel at her job and let her accomplishments speak for themselves.

When asked about the challenges of being a woman in such a high-stakes role, Susie was often candid. "It's not about breaking the glass ceiling just for the sake of it," she said in one interview. "It's about doing the job well, about showing that anyone—man or woman—can lead effectively with the right skills and commitment. I'm here to do the work, not to make statements. If my presence here encourages others, then I'm grateful. But at the end of the day, this role is about serving the country."

Her words resonated with many, especially young women who saw in her an example of what was possible in American politics. Susie became a source of inspiration, not only for her ability to navigate the challenges of her role but for her steadfast focus on results over recognition. She often received messages from women in politics, business, and other fields, expressing gratitude for her leadership and asking for advice on how to succeed in male-dominated industries. In response, Susie often encouraged them to stay true to their principles, to focus on building expertise, and to remain resilient in the face of challenges.

"Don't let anyone tell you that you're here just to fill a quota," she would say to them. "Your place is earned through your work and your dedication. Always remember that."

As Chief of Staff, Susie faced numerous high-stakes decisions that required careful consideration and a balanced approach. One of her primary focuses was to streamline the administration's communication strategy, ensuring that the President's message was clear, consistent, and aligned with the values that had resonated with voters. She implemented regular briefing sessions to keep all departments informed and foster a sense of cohesion, recognizing that internal alignment was essential for effective governance. Her efforts paid off, as the administration's message became more unified, allowing for a stronger, more focused agenda.

In addition to her work within the White House, Susie also maintained relationships with key stakeholders outside of the administration. She frequently engaged with members of Congress, state leaders, and representatives from various interest groups, fostering connections that were essential to advancing the administration's policies. Her ability to navigate these relationships with tact and respect earned her a reputation as a Chief of Staff who was not only effective within the White House walls but also adept at managing the broader political landscape.

However, her tenure was not without its crises. From unexpected policy challenges to urgent international developments, Susie was often called upon to provide guidance and support during critical moments. Her approach was always one of calm assessment, followed by decisive action. She understood that in the Chief of Staff role, hesitation could lead to confusion, and she prioritized clear, timely decision-making to keep the administration on course. Her colleagues admired her ability to think strategically, even under pressure, and her knack for finding solutions where others saw obstacles.

One of her colleagues remarked, "Susie has this gift for seeing the big picture without getting lost in the details. She's always a few steps ahead, thinking about what's next, what could go wrong, and how to handle it. That's what makes her so effective in this role."

In the months following her appointment, Susie's impact became increasingly visible. The White House operated with a renewed sense of purpose, driven by her leadership and the systems she put in place. Her work as Chief of Staff was challenging, often grueling, but she approached each day with the same dedication that had defined her career. To her, this role was an opportunity not only to make history but to contribute meaningfully to the country's future.

Reflecting on her position, Susie remained humble about her achievements. "It's a privilege to be here," she said in a rare personal moment with her team. "But it's also a responsibility. Every decision we make affects people's lives. That's something I never take lightly."

Her historic role as the first woman Chief of Staff served as a testament to her capabilities, her resilience, and her commitment to her work. Susie Wiles had built a career on quiet influence and behind-the-scenes strategy, but in this position, she found herself in the spotlight, setting an example for future generations. Her tenure reminded those around her that true leadership is about integrity, focus, and a willingness to face challenges head-on.

For Susie, breaking new ground wasn't about accolades; it was about showing up every day, putting in the work, and making a difference. Her legacy as the first woman Chief of Staff would stand as a beacon for those who would follow, proving that barriers are meant to be broken, not for recognition but for the progress they enable.

# Chapter 11: Personal Life and Legacy

Throughout her career, Susie Wiles has been known as a formidable political strategist, a woman of rare insight and resilience who has helped shape some of the most consequential campaigns in modern American history. Yet, behind the scenes, away from the press briefings and campaign rallies, Susie has lived a personal life that, by design, remains largely private. She's a figure of contrasts—a person who thrives in the charged atmosphere of political strategy but who also values a quieter, more introspective side of life. Her ability to balance a high-stakes career with her personal values speaks to the complexity of her character and the principles that have guided her through decades of political turbulence.

Susie's friends describe her as someone who approaches personal relationships with the same thoughtfulness that defines her professional life. Although she is known for her ability to navigate political relationships with finesse, she treasures the relationships that have been constants in her life, particularly her family and a small circle of close friends who have remained by her side through the ups and downs of her career. To those who know her well, she is not the intense, calculating strategist often depicted in the media; she's a dedicated mother, a loyal friend, and a woman who, despite her success, remains deeply grounded.

One close friend recounts a telling moment from early in Susie's career: "We were sitting at dinner after one of her first big campaign wins, and everyone was celebrating, congratulating her on this huge accomplishment. But she was mostly quiet, just taking it all in. I asked her why she wasn't more excited, and she said, 'Because tomorrow, we start all over again.' That's Susie—always thinking ahead but never losing sight of what matters to her."

Family has always been a central pillar in Susie's life. Her children and grandchildren are, in her words, her "true legacy," and she has always made an effort to remain present in their lives despite the demands of her career. Balancing her role as a mother and grandmother with her responsibilities as a political strategist has not always been easy, but she prioritizes these relationships as a source of personal fulfillment and stability. Her family's support has been a constant, providing her with a sense of grounding even during the most chaotic times in her career.

For Susie, maintaining this balance has required a conscious effort to keep her work life and personal life separate. She's known to set boundaries, not allowing the pressures of her career to intrude on time with her family. It's a boundary that, she admits, can be challenging to enforce, especially in a field where work often spills over into evenings, weekends, and holidays. But over the years, she's learned to protect her personal time, knowing that her effectiveness as a strategist—and as a person—depends on her ability to recharge and stay connected to the people she loves.

"I've missed a few family dinners, more than a few birthdays," she once acknowledged in a rare personal interview. "But I've also learned when to say no, when to put the phone down, and just be present. My work is important to me, but my family is my foundation."

Another close friend describes Susie as someone who brings the same dedication to her personal life as she does to her professional one. She's a voracious reader, particularly of history and literature, and she often finds solace in books as a way to unwind. While her work involves constant travel and public engagement, Susie finds comfort in small, quiet moments—reading with her grandchildren, spending time outdoors, and, whenever possible, cooking for her family. These moments remind her of what truly matters and give her the strength to return to her demanding career with renewed energy.

But balancing her high-profile career with her personal values hasn't always been easy, particularly when it comes to her core beliefs. As a strategist, Susie has often had to work with candidates and causes that don't fully align with her personal views. It's a reality she approaches pragmatically, understanding that her role is to serve the campaign rather than her own ideals. Still, there have been moments when this disconnect has weighed on her, leading her to reflect on her role in a profession where ideals and strategy often clash.

One colleague recalls a conversation they had during a particularly difficult campaign. "I asked her if she ever struggled with the direction the campaign was taking, and she said, 'Sometimes. But at the end of the day, my job is to advise, to provide the best strategy I can. It's not my place to shape every decision—that's for the candidate.' She has this way of reconciling her role with her values, but I know it's not always easy for her."

In many ways, Susie's legacy is as much about her approach to life as it is about her achievements. Her quiet determination, her resilience, and her unwavering sense of purpose have inspired those around her. She's seen by many as a mentor, a woman who has broken barriers in a field that remains challenging for women, particularly at the highest levels. Younger colleagues often seek her advice, not only on strategy but on how to navigate the complexities of a career in politics without losing oneself in the process.

"Be patient, be persistent, and always remember who you are," she often advises those just starting in their careers. "This work can be all-consuming, but you have to know when to step back and find your center. That's what will keep you grounded."

As Susie reflects on her career, she does so with a sense of gratitude and humility. She's aware of the impact she's had, the victories she's helped secure, and the influence she's wielded, often from behind the scenes. But she's quick to point out that her career is only part of her story. To her, true success isn't measured in campaign victories or titles held—it's found in the relationships she's built, the principles she's upheld, and the family she's cherished.

Her friends and family know that, for all her professional accomplishments, Susie's most enduring legacy will be the values she embodies. She's someone who has shown that it's possible to succeed without compromising one's integrity, that strength can be quiet, and that the truest form of power lies in remaining true to oneself. In a field where loyalty is often conditional and alliances are temporary, Susie has built a career that stands as a testament to commitment, consistency, and character.

As she looks toward the future, Susie remains focused on what she describes as her "real work"—being present for her family, continuing to mentor the next generation of political strategists, and contributing to causes that reflect her values. She's not interested in writing memoirs or seeking recognition; to her, the legacy she leaves is one that lives on in the lives she's touched, the campaigns she's shaped, and the example she's set for those who will follow.

"I've had a good run," she says with a smile, looking back on a career that has taken her from local campaigns to the highest levels of American politics. "But the work I'm most proud of? That's the work I do every day when I'm with my family, when I'm helping someone find their path, when I'm staying true to the things that matter to me. That's my legacy, and that's enough."

In a world that often values ambition over authenticity, Susie Wiles stands out as a reminder that success is not about accolades or power—it's about staying grounded, remaining true to one's values, and finding fulfillment in the journey rather than the destination. Her life, both personal and professional, serves as a guide for those who seek to make a difference without losing themselves along the way. And as she continues to walk her path, she does so with the quiet strength that has always defined her, leaving a legacy that will endure long after the campaigns have ended and the headlines have faded.

# Chapter 12: Reflections and Lessons

Susie Wiles has spent decades in the political trenches, her career marked by high-stakes campaigns, historic wins, and quiet influence behind the scenes. As she reflects on her journey, she is deeply aware of the lessons each experience has offered her—not only about the world of politics but also about the qualities and principles that are essential for anyone who wants to make a meaningful impact in this field. Her insights are both practical and philosophical, grounded in years of hard-won experience and a commitment to staying true to herself, even in the face of shifting alliances and relentless public scrutiny.

For Susie, the first and most enduring lesson has always been the importance of resilience. Politics is not for the faint of heart; it is a field defined by victories and defeats, where every decision can come under intense scrutiny, and where loyalty is often conditional. From her earliest roles in local campaigns to her recent high-profile work on national stages, she's learned that the ability to persevere in the face of challenges is as crucial as any strategic skill.

"Resilience isn't just about bouncing back after a loss," she explains to young strategists seeking her guidance. "It's about maintaining your focus and not letting the noise get to you. People are going to question your motives, doubt your decisions, and challenge your approach. You have to be strong enough to stay steady, to trust your instincts even when others don't."

Her perspective on resilience is practical, shaped by her years of navigating difficult campaigns and contentious issues. For Susie, resilience also means knowing when to step back, reassess, and adapt. In the fast-paced world of politics, where situations can change overnight, she has learned that flexibility is key. While some might interpret resilience as stubbornness, she sees it as an ability to hold on to one's core principles while remaining open to new approaches. "You don't have to change who you are to adapt," she often says. "You just have to be willing to grow."

Another lesson Susie values deeply is the importance of authenticity. In a field often associated with image crafting and spin, she has always believed that the best strategy is honesty. Her approach to working with candidates has been to encourage them to be themselves, rather than trying to fit a mold of what they think a politician should be. Her belief is that voters are more perceptive than they're often given credit for, and that they respond to genuine, straightforward communication.

"People can tell when you're not being real," she says, "and they don't like it. Voters are looking for leaders they can trust, people who understand their lives and their struggles. They want to know who you are, not just what you think they want to hear."

Susie's focus on authenticity doesn't mean that she overlooks the importance of messaging or public image; rather, she sees them as tools that should serve a candidate's true personality and values, not obscure them. In her view, the role of a strategist is to bring out the best in a candidate, to help them connect with voters in a way that feels natural and honest. This approach has not only earned her the respect of those she's worked with but has also become a hallmark of her legacy as a strategist.

Reflecting on the changing landscape of American politics, Susie often speaks about the importance of adaptability. The political world today is vastly different from the one she entered years ago. Social media has transformed the way campaigns are run, bringing new challenges and opportunities. Information moves faster than ever, and public opinion can shift with a single tweet. For Susie, the ability to adapt to these changes without losing one's strategic focus is essential.

"Politics moves at a different pace now," she observes. "It's faster, more intense, and there's less room for error. But at the same time, the fundamentals haven't changed. You still have to understand people, listen to them, and give them a reason to believe in your candidate. The tools might be different, but the principles are the same."

Her advice to young strategists entering this fast-evolving landscape is to embrace new technologies and methods but to always keep their core values in sight. In a world of viral moments and instant feedback, she believes that staying grounded in one's purpose is what makes a strategist effective and respected. "Learn the tools," she advises, "but don't let them define you. Technology is just a means to connect with people. It's your message and your integrity that will ultimately make the impact."

One of the most significant lessons Susie shares is the importance of humility and collaboration. Despite her success, she remains acutely aware that political victories are rarely achieved alone. Behind every win is a team of people, each contributing their expertise, energy, and perspective. Over the years, she has come to value the contributions of every team member, from senior advisors to junior staffers, recognizing that a successful campaign is built on the dedication of many.

"Leadership isn't about being the loudest voice in the room," she often tells her team. "It's about listening, understanding, and respecting the people you work with. Everyone brings something to the table, and it's my job to make sure their voices are heard."

Her emphasis on collaboration is one of the reasons she is admired by those who work with her. Colleagues describe her as someone who values their input, who doesn't just issue directives but engages in meaningful dialogue, encouraging ideas and feedback. For Susie, collaboration is more than just good management; it's a reflection of her belief that the best decisions are those informed by diverse perspectives.

Another key lesson that Susie imparts to those she mentors is the importance of boundaries and balance. Politics is a demanding field that can consume one's life, often at the expense of personal relationships and well-being. Susie is candid about the toll her career has taken, acknowledging that she's missed important family moments and sacrificed personal time in pursuit of her professional goals. Yet, she has also learned the importance of setting boundaries, of knowing when to step back and recharge.

"You can't pour from an empty cup," she reminds her mentees. "Take care of yourself, spend time with your family, and make sure you have something in your life that isn't about politics. It's easy to get caught up in the work, but if you don't have balance, you won't be effective in the long run."

Susie's reflections on balance resonate with many young people in politics who are grappling with the demands of the field. Her willingness to speak openly about the personal side of her journey offers them a reminder that success doesn't have to come at the cost of one's well-being. She encourages them to pursue their goals passionately but to remember that they are more than their careers.

As she considers her legacy, Susie is proud of the impact she has made but remains humble about her accomplishments. To her, success isn't defined by titles or headlines; it's about the relationships she's built, the trust she's earned, and the lives she's touched. Her career is a testament to the power of staying true to one's values, of leading with integrity, and of knowing when to stand firm and when to adapt.

"Legacy isn't about what you leave behind in terms of fame or accolades," she reflects. "It's about the difference you've made in people's lives, the example you've set, and the values you've stood for. If I can look back and see that I've helped people grow, that I've stayed true to who I am, then that's a legacy I'm proud of."

Her advice to future political strategists is simple but profound: "Be patient, be resilient, and don't lose sight of why you're here. Politics isn't just about power—it's about serving people, about working for something bigger than yourself. Never forget that."

In a world where politics is often seen as a ruthless game, Susie Wiles's reflections stand as a reminder of what is possible when one leads with purpose, integrity, and compassion. Her legacy will endure not only in the campaigns she has shaped but in the lives of those she has mentored, inspired, and encouraged to pursue a career in politics with an open heart and a clear mind. And as she passes on her wisdom to the next generation, Susie's words and example continue to light the way for those who will follow in her footsteps, ensuring that her impact will be felt for years to come.

# Epilogue: The Lasting Impact of a Power Broker

Susie Wiles's career stands as a testament to the power of strategy, resilience, and quiet influence in American politics. Over the years, her name has become synonymous with success, trustworthiness, and an ability to navigate the complexities of both local and national campaigns. She has built a legacy that stretches beyond individual victories, leaving an indelible mark on the people and the profession she has dedicated her life to. In a world where public recognition often translates to power, Susie's influence has been one that thrived largely out of the spotlight—a conscious choice, and one that has allowed her to work effectively, with a clear focus on results rather than accolades.

Her lasting impact is evident in the numerous campaigns she's managed, the candidates she's guided to victory, and the future generations of strategists she has inspired. Through her work, she has demonstrated that political influence doesn't necessarily require a prominent public profile; instead, it can be wielded effectively from behind the scenes, with purpose, precision, and a profound understanding of people. To those who know her well, Susie is not only a skilled strategist but also a dedicated mentor and a respected colleague—someone who has built her reputation on trust, discretion, and a relentless commitment to her craft.

Throughout her career, Susie's influence has been rooted in her ability to see beyond the surface. She understands the power of messaging, of connecting with voters on an emotional level, and of crafting campaigns that resonate deeply with the concerns of the electorate. Her approach to politics has always been grounded in a straightforward, people-centered strategy that places the needs and aspirations of the public above party or ideology. This focus on people is perhaps her most lasting legacy, a reflection of her belief that politics, at its core, is about serving the public and understanding the issues that shape their lives.

For Susie, her legacy goes beyond the titles and positions she has held; it is reflected in the impact she has had on the lives of those she has worked with, guided, and inspired. Many young strategists look to her as a role model—a person who has navigated the political world with integrity, grace, and a steadfast dedication to excellence. Her influence can be seen in the way she has helped shape a new generation of political operatives who are not only skilled in strategy but also committed to the values she embodies:

resilience, authenticity, and a deep respect for the people they serve.

One of Susie's closest colleagues reflects on her legacy with admiration: "Susie never did this work for the recognition. She's always been about the work itself—the challenge, the complexity, the opportunity to make a difference. That's why she's so respected. People know they can trust her to be honest, to be steady, and to always put the mission first."

Her reputation as a "power broker" comes not only from the influence she wields but also from the consistency and reliability she brings to each campaign and candidate. In an industry often marked by shifting loyalties and fleeting alliances, Susie has been a stabilizing force, a professional who values the integrity of her work and the trust of those she serves. Her career reflects a deep-seated belief in the importance of loyalty—to her team, to her candidates, and to her own standards of excellence.

As she continues to build on her legacy, Susie remains committed to her work and to the principles that have defined her career. She is not one to rest on her laurels or to view past successes as a reason to slow down. Instead, she sees each new challenge as an opportunity to refine her approach, to deepen her understanding, and to leave an even greater impact on the field. For her, the work is ongoing, a lifelong pursuit of excellence and a continuous journey of growth.

In addition to her professional achievements, Susie's legacy is also characterized by the relationships she has fostered and the people she has mentored along the way. She has always been generous with her time and her knowledge, understanding that the strength of a legacy lies not only in personal accomplishments but in the ways one empowers others to succeed. To the many young strategists she has guided, Susie is more than a mentor; she is an example of what it means to navigate a career in politics with integrity and purpose.

"Susie taught me that it's not about the wins and losses; it's about how you play the game," one former mentee says. "She showed me that true influence comes from doing the work well, from staying focused, and from never compromising your values. That's something I'll carry with me for the rest of my career."

Her impact reaches beyond individual campaigns and into the broader political landscape, where her contributions have helped shape the strategies and standards that define modern campaigning. Through her work, she has shown that politics can be a noble profession, one that has the power to effect real change when approached with sincerity and a genuine commitment to the public good. Her legacy is a reminder that behind every campaign slogan, every public appearance, and every election result, there are people like Susie Wiles—dedicated professionals who devote themselves to the intricate and often unseen work of democracy.

As she looks to the future, Susie remains focused on what she describes as her "life's mission": to make a positive impact, to help shape a more effective political process, and to continue guiding others who share her commitment to public service. Her influence may not always be visible, but it is deeply felt, resonating through the campaigns she has led, the candidates she has mentored, and the countless lives she has touched along the way.

Reflecting on her career, Susie speaks with a sense of gratitude and purpose. "I've been fortunate to do work that I believe in, to help people who want to make a difference, and to be part of something bigger than myself. That's all I ever wanted—to leave things a little better than I found them."

Her words reflect the essence of her legacy: a quiet but powerful dedication to making a difference, not for personal gain but for the good of others. As the years go by, Susie Wiles's influence will undoubtedly continue to shape American politics, her name spoken not for its flashiness but for the respect it commands. And though she may not seek the limelight, her legacy will endure as a testament to the impact one can have through hard work, humility, and an unwavering commitment to doing what is right.

For future generations of political strategists, Susie's career offers a blueprint for success that is defined not by fame or fortune but by integrity, purpose, and a dedication to the principles that transcend individual campaigns. Her story is a reminder that true power lies not in the spotlight but in the quiet, determined work that makes meaningful change possible.

In the end, Susie Wiles's legacy will not be measured by headlines or accolades but by the trust she has earned, the lives she has influenced, and the positive change she has helped create. And as she continues her work, she remains a steady, guiding force—a testament to what can be achieved through commitment, perseverance, and an unwavering dedication to the people she serves. This is the lasting impact of a power broker who has quietly, yet indelibly, shaped the course of American politics.